UNBROKEN CIRCLE, UNENDING THREAD

Filled with well-crafted radiance and gratitude, James K. Zimmerman's *Unbroken Circle, Unending Thread* is a poetry collection that not only sings but understands how to listen as well, whether to "the internal rhyme / of pink and / crimson azaleas" or "the unending heartbeat / of wintering trees." With humor, precision, and the lightest of touches, Zimmerman finds inspiration in the cycle of seasons, birds, blossoms, even murderous black cats and trespassing deer. Here are poems that invite readers to slow down, breathe deeply, and take notice of the delicate splendor that surrounds us—the circle and thread that binds us all.

—Jared Harél
author of *Let Our Bodies Change the Subject*

James K. Zimmerman's poems express the textures and sounds of the natural world—"rowdy raspberry canes / that scratch their names"—and describe diverse creatures, including the human narrator who is "on a first name basis / with every stem of kale … in the little garden." Reading these lyrical, precise, and highly attuned depictions, we come to understand what the red-tail hawk knows: that "lawns are not to be / overflown, but examined / with a poet's eye."

—Hilary Sallick
author of *Love Is a Shore*

In this collection of stunning poems imbued with tenderness, wit, and wisdom, James K. Zimmerman takes us with him on a journey through the life cycle of a year. Each poem expresses the depth of his connection to the rhythms of the seasons. By no means are these poems maudlin or naïve, however; throughout, there is the background hum of concern for our planet, the voice of climate change. I sit in wonder as I read these poems, witnessing how the poet bows to our nonhuman companions, even in our fraught Anthropocene epoch. His deep respect for the oak, the hawk, the mantis, and the rose, for all of the natural world, calls us to honor our place in that world, to resist the belief that we are separate from it.

—Judith Sarah Schmidt, Ph.D.
author of *Blessing from Broken*

"I was on a first-name basis / with every stem of kale," James K. Zimmerman tells us. Intimacy, identification, care-full attention—these qualities saturate this enlivening collection. Newly hatched spiders are "scurrying punctuation points"; a mockingbird is a "jazz riffer in the key of wings." As he builds this book around the four seasons, the effects of global warming can't be avoided. But it's as critical to observe and report the breath and pulse of each individual day. Anthropomorphic imagery is here, too—"snowbound hollies bow / downward-dog to sunset" as one delightful example. It's not to explain other beings as just like us, though, but to propose ways for us to understand them. We need all the help with that we can get. And how could my jaw not drop at "lawn chairs strewn around / the yard like dead chickens or kids / sleeping it off after karaoke night"? Read *Unbroken Circle, Unending Thread* to rediscover what you didn't know you knew.

—DAVID P. MILLER
author of *Bend in the Stair* and *Sprawled Asleep*

In *Unbroken Circle, Unending Thread,* James K. Zimmerman takes us on a journey around the sun, through the seasons, into the personas of a black widow spider, an oak tree, ladybug, praying mantis, a mockingbird. In one poem, a loon reveals its thoughts: "You are in my world / not I in yours;" "I slide into/the water's womb/like a thought slipping/into mind." Birds are a frequent presence, as are many deer and one fox who arrives as an unexpected guest at an outdoor wedding.

These poems transport us—in time and place. Reading in summer, I felt the welcome cold of a snowy winter, could hear the crunch of boots on ice, imagine maples without leaves. Through his poems, I enjoyed a beach in Mexico, tiny turtles released to the surf. Zimmerman's well-crafted lines create a universe we can recognize, in which we feel at home. He teaches us to see, newly; a modern world, yet peering into wildness.

—LAURA FOLEY
author of *Sledding the Valley of the Shadow*

UNBROKEN CIRCLE, UNENDING THREAD

James K. Zimmerman

Fernwood
PRESS

Unbroken Circle, Unending Thread

Fernwood Press
Newberg, Oregon
www.fernwoodpress.com

Printed in the United States of America

Cover and page design: Mareesa Fawver Moss
Cover photo: James K. Zimmerman
Author photo: Daniel Topete

ISBN 978-1-59498-217-0

To Dhiravamsa, who nurtured by example my nascent need to see with new eyes.

To Jan and Chloe, who know my light and my shadows, the turning of my seasons, my deepest love.

Le véritable voyage de découverte ne consiste pas à chercher de nouveaux paysages, mais à avoir de nouveaux yeux, de voir l'univers avec les yeux d'un autre, de cent autres, de voir les cent univers que chacun d'eux voit, que chacun d'eux est.

The true journey of discovery does not consist of seeking new landscapes, but to have new eyes, to see the universe with the eyes of another, of a hundred others, to see the hundred universes that each of them sees, that each of them is.

—from *La Prisonnière,* the fifth volume of Marcel Proust's
À la recherche du temps perdu (*In Search of Lost Time*)

Instructions for living a life:

Pay attention.
Be astonished.
Tell about it.

—from "Sometimes," in Mary Oliver,
Red Bird (Beacon, 2008)

Contents

Thanks

Thanks to Eric Muhr and the staff at Fernwood, without whose support and shepherding this book would never have found its way to appearance in print.

Thanks to my writing colleagues and fellow workshoppers, whose incisive comments and suggestions enrich and hone my voice.

Thanks to my father, Howard Zimmerman, for teaching me how to fish, and to my mother, Joanne Kuper Zimmerman, for showing me how things grow in the earth and on the page.

Thanks to the seasons and all the creatures—animate and otherwise—who compelled me to listen to their voices, their stories, and whose lives have inspired my spirit for as long as I can remember.

Acknowledgments

Grateful acknowledgement is made to the following journals, in which these poems first appeared, sometimes in earlier versions:

Assisi: "Penance"
Atlanta Review: "Second Chance"
Avocet: "I Wait for Winter to Begin"
Blueline: "Incantation: Splitting Maple," "Winter Song Cycle," "This Morning, Snow"
Chicago Quarterly Review: "Teach a Man to Fish"
Cloudbank: "Snowshoeing Mt. Tom"
Common Ground: "Nurturance," "The Loon God of Megunticook Lake"
Ellipsis: "La La La the Life Goes On"
Evansville Review: "Black Widow"
Freshwater: "Cold Snap"
Hawai'i Pacific Review: "Exit Ramp"
Inkwell: "How to Birth a Perfect Pear"
Leaping Clear: "Incantation: Felling Ash," "Incantation: Stacking Oak"
Mochila Review: "Wedding Party, Winter Park"
Nimrod: "Wormholes of the White-Tail Deer"
New England Poetry Club: "This Is the End of Winter, This Is the Beginning"

Off Channel: "Sparrow Logic"
Pinyon: "Good Fences," "Heirloom"
Pleiades: "Praying Mantis"
Poetry Port: "Mockingbird"
Reed: "The Dilemma Regarding the Murderous Black Cat"
Salt: "Wednesday (Winter Solstice)"
Sky Island: "Anasazi"
Snapdragon: "Solace (April 7, 10 AM)"
SN Review: "Icicles"
Stone Poetry Quarterly: "Arachnophilia"
The Cape Rock: "Symbiosis"
The Kerf: "Mid-April Morning Mash-Up," "Autobiography of a Dying Oak"
The Worcester Review: "Harvest (December 13)"
Third Wednesday: "Ladybug"
Tipton Poetry Journal: "Central Beach (Indiana Dunes)"
Trajectory: "Elegy for the Leaves"
Urthona: "Goldfinches," "Solstice"
Voices: "Photographic Memory"
Wild Leaf Press: "Lifeblood"
Willows Wept Review: "Thanksgiving Day"

Thanks also to *Outermost Community Radio* for awarding the Joe Gouveia Prize to "The Loon God of Megunticook Lake," *Cloudbank* for awarding the Cloudbank Poetry Award to "Snowshoeing Mt. Tom," and the *New England Poetry Club* for presenting the E.E. Cummings Prize to "This Is the End of Winter, This Is the Beginning."

I. WINTER

Hudson Valley, Christmas Eve

barefoot
I go out to feed
the birds

they wonder why
they are still here

raindrops tap
my T-shirt
on the shoulder

a sodden maple leaf
wraps around my foot

like a bow

This Morning, Snow

began to fall sleepily
each flake a mandala

kaleidoscopic
in the early light

inviting me to fall
with it, become frozen
ground below

now it blows with blinding
speed, ten thousand
voices speaking as one

a Greek chorus
foreshadowing silence

Cold Snap

hung from a bare limb
of the old sugar maple, the feeder
lay fallow these past four days

the snowed-in silence held me
in quiet awe, but held me
back, too cold, I thought

sparrows and chickadees
choosing a warmer place
to face the bitter soul of winter

today, the solitude breaks
in a hint of thaw, speaks
in drips and crunches

though the wind still whips
from eyes to feet like the sudden
smack of a gunshot

I go out in only mocs and hood
to do penance, to greet the snow
the sound of breath and footfall

bring the feeder in, fill its hunger
with millet, black sunflower seeds
and a handful of peanuts

brave the shards of wind
once more, hook the feeder
over the maple's waiting arm

and come back to the roasting
chicken fragrance of the kitchen
still hushed by the chill

I sit at a window rimed in lines
of frost, and within a minute
or two, a cardinal reappears

brilliant against the snow
like the drop of blood in the heart
of Queen Anne's lace, cracks

a sunflower seed, signal
to chickadees and sparrows
hopeful in their overcoats

they arrive in a quickening
of wings, a clatter of chirps
in chorus, a shiver of song

Rockwood Hall in Winter

the horse-and-buggy lane speaks
softer now under cloven stagprint
fractured branch and Vibram sole

only the snowswept field
recalls in tacit witness
languid lawn soirees that reveled
in champagne splendor

the nearby formal garden wall
still turns away in stern reproach
the rowdy raspberry canes
that scratch their names in its face

even the prideful veranda
staring downhill to the river
and the setting sun is now
eclipsed by greedy branches
of beech and maple unleashed
from the landscape gardener's
careful, calloused hand

no hubris lurking here, no hope
of resurrection save perhaps
through gravid deer in spring
droopy fruited canes in summer
the river freed again from
the memory of winter ice

Snowshoeing Mt. Tom

the timeworn path rises to greet me
in crunch and flurry, slowing
my unheedingly hurried pace
to a rhythm at one with the flow
of breath and receding thought

here in the early afternoon sunlight
some would call lemon yellow
that is closer perhaps
to tarnished heirloom silver
I see the trees as a forest

while maples red and sugar
and pines white and black
know the forest is a hillside village

here in the open mind of silence
I hear the path as a bloodline
veining itself through the skin
on the back of the hand of earth

while Norway spruce and white ash
see me as a solitary blurred moment
and black pine and red maple hear me
as the murmur of a recollected
dream forgotten once again

and so I say: when I am ready to die
bring me here to the forest
and leave me to wait in rhythm
with the unending heartbeat
of wintering trees

Infestation

these days, I often find
knuckleprints of white-
tail deer—carriers of lithe
ethereal beauty and zoonotic
viral load—in the snow

the arbor vitae are at risk

once I was able to keep
their prehensile lips
and grinding molars at bay
with a low green fence

their sandpaper tongues
and delicate nostrils away
with the putrescence of
rotten eggs and garlic

their hypersonic ears
pained by the windy clash
of pie-plates suspended
from sinewy limbs
of the bushes themselves

but the deer have overcome
all that, worked an end-
around, grown steelier
olfactory nerves, stopples
for their ears in preparation

for a crepuscular assault
on newborn needle-tips
that only ventured out
last October—no

there is no immunity to this

Good Fences

through the fog of breath I see
my neighbor, much older now
with tremor and shuffle, struggling
on icy steps to the railing at his door

although there is no fence between us
he would have addressed me curtly
years ago, in full voice, about my snow
on his lawn, threatening a police report
if my dog came too close, wagging
in his creeping juniper

but perhaps he has forgotten all that
his memory these days like branches
of forsythia hidden under last week's storm

when I wave, he offers a raspy hello
and when I speak about the cold
in the darkening afternoon, he agrees

my shoveling over, I think to offer him
a little help with his front walk
but I hesitate, then turn away

knowing he needs the last
of his pride and dignity
and would say no thank you
from behind his leafless birch

Icicles

on the eaves, icicles cannot decide
whether to stay
or go
relentlessly they drip
a heartbeat
too fast to be a ticking clock
too slow to dance
too unsteady to be
an accountant

at first it was
soldiers marching
proud white gloves gripping
bayoneted rifles

then a roofer
slamming one last nail
to keep winter from rushing in

and last a writer at her keyboard
hammering out the final chapter
of her life's story
before the blood runs out

or is it stiff, impatient fingers
thrumming on the windowpane
willing me to wake up?

but no
it is simply
time
speaking through icicles
breathing

trying to decide whether to stay

or go

February 21, 77° Fahrenheit

lambent clouds play freeze tag
among branches relieved of last
week's glassine sleeves of ice

like vegans at a pig roast, no one
quite knows what to make of this

when I fill the feeder, winter birds
say *no thanks, I'm on a low-carb diet*
their hungry eyes in search of sleepy
grubs and earthworms instead

unsure what to sniff first, rich smells
of earth, spoor, and rabbits rising
to his twitching nose, the black lab
wonders *where's the white stuff?*
where's the white stuff?

in confusion, oak and maple logs
wait impatiently on the woodpile
for their turn to burn away the chill
of an unexpected blizzard

how much time do you think
we have to hang around? they ask
feeling sodden rot begin to crawl
into their cambium

and I, I know I should be grateful
for this shorts-and-T-shirt afternoon
but still I feel a pressing need
to shield my eyes from the sun's
unrelenting glare

Autobiography of a Dying Oak

yes, I syphon lifeblood
from the soil beneath me
and yes, I draw it up
through arteries, through
xylem, to feed my proud
young branches, silver
threads in a verdant crown

and yes, they grapple
with the wind, grasp
the sun, the rarity of air

and yes, I mark my days
in cambium, my girth
in annular rings, annals
of my dialogue with snow
with rain, with years
of thirsty earth

and yes, my bare-knuckle roots
insinuate through rocks
push pebbles to the side
burrow like a snake through
clay and limestone, keepers
of the footprints of millennia

and yes, I breathe out
as you breathe in

but only when I crack and
crash to earth, or when you
vivisect me for your hearth
will you learn of wounds
I could not heal, knotholes
full of squirrel dung
trunk lines where the grain
is twisted, memories I have
tried so hard to erase

like names of summer lovers
tattooed on my seeping skin

Sacrament

snowbound hollies bow
downward-dog to sunset

ice binds their boughs
like buckets of cement
to punish them for last
year's exuberance

under unforgiving weight
they plead for warmth
in the arctic earth below

I leave my hat and gloves
at the door, sainted hero
that I am, bring my old
straw broom along

and jab, slash, sweep, shove
'til laden branches rise again

squirrels chatter, jays panic
frantic to see their alpine
wonderland upended

but the hollies, in gratitude
whip my face with scrawny
claws, bless my hands
with jagged scratches, blood
mingling with bitter sap

once again, we share
this annual sacrament:

last rites for winter snow
evensong for the advent
of spring

Lifeblood

last night
though it tasted of early snow
the sky had the stark clarity
of unexpected insight, the moon
proudly wore its foreboding stare
and clouds, trembling acolytes
reflected its stern rebuke

still
there was a softness in the mist
winter more kindly old dowager
than icy dominatrix, and along
the road, streetlights winked
in sequence, candles at a party
waiting on the cake

today
birds pour down like rain
in sparrow chirp, blue jay
squawk, and robin tittering
awaken hungry brown grass
alert trees to begin their flow
of sap, lifeblood
of the neighborhood

a solo flicker, bugler at reveille
bangs its jackhammer head
against the stuporous trunk
of a sugar maple

and now
among empty-handed bushes
a blink-eyed tawny cat
sinuous tail swaying
like a fakir's cobra, licks
its indolent paws

and waits

II. SPRING

I Wait for Winter to Begin

I wait for winter to begin, to weave
    its windy tentacles
through icy earth and sullen sky

to take my inner landscape
    to its darkest place
to train my eye
    on an unseen sun
to turn my face cold
    as an untold secret

so that I may measure
    the coming of spring
in salt tears of forgiveness
        and relief

but no
    this year, winter held me
hostage in brown earth
    absent snow
dripping eaves
        frozen smiles

today
        to no surprise
    it rains again
the equinox has passed
    in unmarked splendor

but still I wait for winter to begin

This Is the End of Winter, This Is the Beginning

I know I should not
pick up by hand this

mess of gray fur, russet
fur. bones. teeth

the holly branch clipped
last fall has waited

here on the ground
since November

survived the white
of snow, the freezing

to be slid under
the carcass, to flip

the shell of life into
the hedge of arbor vitae

I see, I think, a rabbit leg

and look: the lawn
wants to be green

Because of the Buy-One-Get-One-Free Sale

Kohl's, CVS, and Vision World
grudgingly welcome a squabble
of seagulls to their parking lot
today, not willing to upset
seafarers among their clientele
despite no sea or even a puddle
within driving distance

the gulls clatter on a spit
of dirt just inside the curb
beside a Tesla, a Lexus
and a slush of snow

it is a mob scene, seemingly
the only spot where a school
of herring somehow fell
to earth from the height
of a blizzard, the gulls beating
their wings and each other
dozens more circling above

and, as suddenly, they leave
perhaps hearing of a heap
of spoiled meat sunbathing
behind the Stop & Shop
a stoplight away

I sidle over to the wedge
of barren soil that had so
captivated the birds a few
minutes ago and find nothing
to incite their ravenous melee
except the remains of a bag
of Himalayan Sea Salt Doritos
a discarded mask and coupon
for thirty-percent off

as the Tesla silently creeps
away, laden with newfound
treasures and progressive lenses
and the Lexus purrs in self-
satisfaction over a buy-one-
get-one-free sale on toothpaste

Solace (April 7, 10 a.m.)

here today there is
the feel of fall

crisp apple chill
in the gray air

chickadees bemused
by lack of snow

robin sentry-straight
on shingles, orange

flash against the deep
green breath of April rain

iris, lilac, spice
viburnum bleary-eyed

awakening too soon
from winter's sleep

seeking the solace
of summer sun

Red Rose Blues

this petulant rose does not
agree to leaf out again
until the beaks and talons
of winter have flown

so I am never certain
if my solomonic shears
have gone too far—
which stems to take
how close to black earth
before I cause roots
to wither and die

I touch a thorn
and sing, choosing
a paean over a dirge

I know there is always a risk
in growing roses, a balance
between vibrant color
and bleeding fingers
between redolent beauty
and bone-deep scars of loss

so I sing again and wait
to see the blood-red
of new growth as I pare
winter's death away

Mid-April Morning Mash-Up

after my usual dose of thorns
on hands and forearms—
punishment for cutting back
last year's raspberry canes
and dead branches of the tea rose—
it made sense to call the kid
next door and ask him to come over
and teach the lawn a lesson

the grass posing for post-prom
selfies, and little bearded faces
of dandelions poking up
through dry leaves fall left behind

it feels more like May today
though the maples, dogwoods
and lilacs don't know it yet
and the viburnum is sound asleep

robins hang out in the on-deck circle
warming up their beaks, ready
to peck at the dirt with cocked heads
for ticks and drowsy worms

it seems the forsythia alone
in their yellow pinafores know
for sure it is only Good Friday

but then that solo cardinal
on the telephone cable
calls out "here, here"
or is it "hear, hear"?

or maybe just
"listen"

Exit Ramp

at first, two stars
in shadow, eyes
at the side of the road

one hoof upraised
mid-thought, a comma
above the gravel
ears twitching, fallen leaves

I flicker high beam low beam
high low high
holding her there
tail flashing white dark white
no startled leap, no
sudden death

she hesitates, turns
away, supplicant nose
to the ground
leaving the fallen
fawn at her feet

flicker

she will survive this, move on
in shadow
turning away

Arachnophilia

suspended in my field
of vision, a tiny tan
specter on the white
canvas of the door

or a floater
                    detritus
that perplexes
        my retina

but this one moves
on its own
        relying not
                    on the
                        muscles
of my eye

I reach into the air
        aware
of a thing
        I cannot see
                    a thread
that must be there

and grasp it

little creature now
in my control
        or so I think

the line
between us
linked
by finger
thumb
and eight
jittery legs

I drop
        the wriggling
poppy seed
        to the safety
of the floor

go on your way, I say

but as I move a leg
        it tags along
somehow
        spins
                another
unseen strand
        now seeks
my companionship

suddenly
        I am no longer
puppeteer to my micro
        marionette

I shake my hand
        try to let it go
release something
        I have lost
                the thread of

it merges into speckled
        tiles or laces
of my shoe

and now I have lost
the reason why
I stood before the whiteness
of the door
in the first place

Sparrow Logic

the screen door ajar
a sparrow flies in

takes up the whole room

they all stand back
hands over hearts

stand back, they say

I wouldn't do that if I
were you, they say

that bird is wild
            has a disease
doesn't belong to us
            with us here
doesn't know our songs

the sparrow grows
            even larger

so I talk to
            reach for
the bird

I wouldn't do that if I

but if you were, you'd
have no choice but this:

talk to the bird, cup it
in one hand, carry it
                        outside

and show your face
            to the sky

Red-Tail

on my neighbor's careful
yard, a red-tail hawk
dissects a young squirrel
pausing casually between

pulls at the flesh to glance
skyward, contemplating
this realm he reads as closely
as a favorite lyric poem

to him, lawns are not to be
overflown but examined
with a poet's eye:

an iambic breeze
            riffling irises

the internal rhyme
            of pink and
            crimson azaleas

line breaks
            of a flagstone walk

quatrains
            of a picket fence

until one turn of phrase—
a slight movement
near a rosebush—tells
the broad-beamed raptor
exactly where to dive

and when to extend talons
to grasp and savor the fierceness
of the final stanza

This Morning I Remind Myself That Everything Is Relative

not too bad, the storm last night, none
of that train roar we get sometimes
when a front runs through

the neighbor's dog stopped yelping
right around dawn, let me get in
an hour of sleep or so before I saw

the storm knocked the umbrella off
its moorings on the patio, leaned it over
like a mushroom just about to rot

left the lawn chairs strewn around
the yard like dead chickens or kids
sleeping it off after karaoke night

but funny, it didn't seem too bad
didn't hear the rain spewing hip-hop
or thunder playing snare and kick drum

maybe just the hi-hat hiss and snap
when a couple of shingles flew off
the back roof and landed in the hedge

not as bad as the time when
the old oak next door heaved itself
over the fence at the garage

and it looked like the conduit
bringing in the power pulled away
from the siding but no, it was

the old oak pushed the garage
off its foundation in a rage
and that time the neighbor
couldn't get his dog to shut up

Solstice

I ate a strawberry
from my garden today

picked it well before
it was really ripe

there were only three
                    and this one
was most nearly
all red with little
wisps of winter white

I wanted to keep it
safe from rabbits
squirrels and dirty-
handed children

the first bite tasted
of cool spring rain

the second of summer's
seductive heat

I will wait for the others
to be almost ready too

III. SUMMER

Mockingbird

jazz riffer in the key of wings
cloaked in a body of morning gray
white shoulder epaulets straight up
and straight-laced like an admiral

but what an ear for the words
other birds cannot easily express
the sweet music you hear
in their pedestrian monotony

yes you are a plagiarist of wren
and robin cardinal chickadee
phoebe sparrow flicker
even crow and whippoorwill

high on the energy
of your own unruly improv
slurring their words twisting
clipping shouting singing them

you are the Sarah the Ella the Miles
the swing scat and bebop to their
singular whistles chirps and squawks

you grab them by the downy throat
and fling their humble stuttering
back at them in stunning flights
of translation and cunning paraphrase

you sing it loud to the skies
as if your life relied upon it
knowing that in fact it does

even when no one shows up
to write the rave reviews

Goldfinches

just now two
goldfinches
on the feeder
brilliance in
yellow and black
elegance among
dun-backed
sparrows and I

ask them how
the chippy
sparrows let
them in with-
out an entrance
fee or full-
throated attack

(no answer too
busy eating) and I

ask them how
it feels to fly
in ecstatic
swoops and dives

(no answer too
busy with millet
and sunflower) and I

ask them do you
really shout
"wheeee" when
you dip and rise

or is it just in my
imagination
and

Photographic Memory

the one photo I lost that day
the one that slipped between
the fingers of the camera
and the eye of the hard drive

between the mist and the meadow
was the one when two great blue
herons held a quiet tête-à-tête

legs thin, straight as a nine iron
origami wings glinted silver-gray
in the latening afternoon

to the whirr of my zoom
pre-Cambrian beaks dipped
to each other in respect or in
contemplation of flashing fish
in the murk at their saurian feet

necks arched, cobras dancing
one behind the other, they created
a perfect Hallmark heart

shutter clicked and got it, I said

I could see the centerfold
in *Natural History*, thousands
of daily hits on YouTube
as they disentangled, slowly
became two again in a careful
effort to be invisible in plain sight

later, in the windswept night
when the evidence was lost
the fish gulped and devoured
the fame green in the gullet
of recollection

the pulse of avian ballet still
shadowed my salt-strewn eyes

The Loon God of Megunticook Lake

you think at first I am
simply a black dot woven
into the mirror mirage
of waveless water—a rock
the head of a beaver
a discarded can of beer

but come closer: I will not
flee, afraid, to the safety
of a distant sky, no

I will turn to you, show
the speckled black
and white of my wings
my back a perfect
Audubon sketch
reflecting the sun's glint
on the skin of the lake

around my neck a lace
Elizabethan collar, etching
of a stand of birch, silver
white on the black
of my head, my eye
a ruby stud, the regal
curve of my beak

you are in my world
now, not I in yours
my bob and drift
ripple and wake

you cannot know
where I will reappear
when I slide into
the water's womb

like a thought slipping
into mind, I re-emerge
in a lily pad tangle
the gulp and belch songs
of hidden bullfrogs

then again fade
into algaic murk, flash
beneath you, a torpedo
drive a school of chum
to riffle the glassy
surface, break the silence
thirty yards away—

laughing

after all, you named
your fits of folly to honor
my haunting call,
harbinger of dusk
and fog, your lunate
fantasy of who I am

but come closer: swim
with me, dive with me
and I will restore your
sacred visions, amniotic
memories, the wildness
of your dreams

Penance

I shake the orange tree
to make the high fruit
                                        fall

two fledglings flung
to the ground
too young to fly

I cradle the smell
of orange blossoms
in bleeding hands

and enshroud myself
                in memory
of the muscularity
of trees I know so well

slick roughness
of black cherry
sinuosity of plum
apple's crotchety agility

and rotting fruit
that finds its way
to cider and brandy
on the ground

Elegy for the Leaves

I was on a first-name basis
with every stem of kale
rainbow chard, and red leaf
lettuce in the little garden
outside my kitchen window

spoke with them daily
sang to them, waited
until the sun hid behind
the house to water them

so droplets—tiny prisms
gatherers of light—
would not turn unfurling
leaves to crêpe and dust

fed them, watched them
flourish, delicate and proud

planned the harvest
at the balance point—
the fulcrum between
leaves too small
and shoots about to bolt—

until today, when I
found among them
a sleek rabbit, rival
admirer and predator
who stared me down

before he slipped away
without a scintilla
of shiver and squeak
cheeks replete
with tender leaves

so I knew it was their time

reverently, I took to them
with scissors and knife,
cutting close enough
to the ground to take

their feathers and their hearts
for myself, but not too close
holding in my hands the hope
they might leaf out again

now I will bathe them
dry them, feel their serrate
edges on my lips, taste
their earthy sweetness
and savor the bitterness
that parches the root
of my tongue

next time I will leave a share
for the rabbit to glean

Wedding Party, Winter Park

he arrives late, materializes
a few sure steps from a lone
white pine in the meadow

coat molting into summer
gray to red, gray to red
tail a plume of smoke
a forgotten thought trailing
at the edge of consciousness

enticed, perhaps, by the foreign
redolence of grilling chicken breasts
sirloin tips, coleslaw, German
chocolate wedding cake

behind the split-rail fence
we greet him, beers in hand

he is now, after all, the interloper
in his own alpine valley

oh look, a fox—a coyote?—
we say in sun-drenched unison
safe in the confines of knowing
what he will do

and on cue, he stops, hesitates
sniffs the wind, turns, pretending
he just remembered the gift
he left at home, trots
window-shopping for lupines

back to the portal in the white pine
where he can dematerialize again

until tonight, when darkness
reclaims our site and bits
of burgers and refried beans
rise to his curious eye
and hungry teeth

Wormholes of the White-Tail Deer

in the forest of my ancient memory
peopled with red maple, white pine
and bee-flowered laurel, they weave
a graceful weft to the warp

of tenacious copses and lacerating
brambles, without a scratch
on ash-golden haunches
candle flames in hazy twilight
phantoms in the fog of dawn

they appear, waver, fade
transported through wormholes
from a timeless alternate universe

when I come too close, say
within the audible crunch
of a twig, a chiseled head

snaps to attention, ears
an early warning system
nostrils flared to seek the musky
scent of a lurking predator

he barks an old man's cough
lifts a wary foreleg, and suddenly
three, five, ten of them spring
into the air, spotted fawns

tawny does, white tails flash
fleeing hooves in staccato rhythm
on hard-packed rocks and clay

guardian, he stands his ground
he is the last to go

and in a flicker of time they melt
into the undergrowth to a parallel
safer world where supple power
and lissome beauty are not harvested
by bullet, arrow, tooth, or claw

but here today, among well-dressed
houses and geometric streets
they stand and stare, sniff the air
as I walk softly by, antlers smug
and sharp in the squinting glare
of the morning sun, daring me
to turn in their direction

they do not shudder, cough, bark
or flick their quickening tails
nor do they thank me for how nicely
I arrange my arbor vitae, irises
carrots, and tomatoes
for their daily ravaging

I think perhaps this fertile plot
this verdant heaven is that
parallel world to which they fled
so many years ago through
a telescopic twist of time

when they turned away and
disappeared, startled at the very sight
and fearsome smell of me

Black Widow

we could not let you rest
suspended from a crazy-
quilt web among peeling
flakes of ceiling, in your
glistening ebony jumpsuit
hourglass the crimson
of new blood, ghost-white
egg case by your side

so we held a pickle jar
below, slid a slip of paper
under your stiletto heels

and impossibly, you fell
egg case still in tow, into
your new brine-scented
home of glass

we fed you carpenter ants
and juicy house flies when
          we caught them

we gave you sun-dried twigs
to help you weave a waiting
          net of silk

in less than three days' time
your tightly lidded house
was overrun with scurrying
punctuation points, three dozen
          if not more

proud mother, already dressed
in black, you gave yourself
to them, devoured, drained
          of life

you rested there, golden
    calf they prayed to
while they learned the skill
so well, paralysis by bite
power of the kill, that

three days on just three
were left to see the rest
suspended from the silken
    quilt, tiny commas

or the lilting rise of a still
    unanswered question

Teach a Man to Fish

give a man a fish, and he will
crave the subtle flavor of sole
scallions and garlic, salmon's
oily meat glazed with soy
and brown sugar, or soft
catfish flesh within the crunch
of deep-fried corn

teach a man to fish, and he will
learn to crave the bobber tucking
under the river's skin like the nod
of a head when a dream tugs
from below the ripples of sleep

and he will wait to savor a rainbow
trout with a barbed hook in its lip
the roiling flash of a school
of cocktail blues, the breach
of a small-mouth bass, or steady
insistence of flounder deep
in the folds of an ocean floor

teach a man to fish, and he will
learn to brave the flop and gasp
the flapping of gills, the sharp slice
through vertebrae just behind the head
the gutting from anus to throat, blood
spattering on deck, dock, shoes

and he will learn to read ripples
on water, the inverse of a breeze's
path, the easy flick of a cast
that lands the lure or bait where
it needs to be, at a sunken log
the seam of a stream, or deep
in the belly of the ocean

teach a man to fish, and if
he is fortunate, he will learn
the quietude of early morning mist
in a birch canoe, evening shadows
under sail, the beauty of the placid
lulls and rolling surges of water
the tranquility of a day on a dock

when nothing takes the hook
at all, and a meal of beans, sunset
and roasted corn satisfies
his craving

Nurturance

on a beach in Mayto—sun
a peeled orange, sand
like turbinado sugar—
we found tiny turtles

groping out of burrows
to head blink-eyed
toward the waves

sometimes crashing surf
tossed them like pebbles
and they landed belly up
feet flailing
in the salt air

so we turned them back over
coaxed them
through the froth
toward the western sun

only one in one hundred
sea turtles survives
oil slicks, satellite microwaves
and sharks to return

twelve years later to lay eggs
in the place
where it was born

they say to guide hatchlings
toward the setting sun
when surf flips them over
can make them forget

how to find their way
back to the beach
of their birth

but we could not stop ourselves:
    we picked them up
and pointed them
    to a fragile future

do you remember?

and suddenly I remembered
    when you took
your first steps
    staggered and fell
surprised to find
    you could rise up again

your hand held my finger
    tight as a talisman
bootied toes heading
    toward the glass
of the patio door

I held your hand
    as you toddled
triumphant, your face
    gleaming
in sunlight

Central Beach (Indiana Dunes)

on the voluptuous pregnant belly
                    of the dunes
children giggle and shriek, gulls
swoop and soar in the graying sunset

teeming masters of mayhem
and cacophony, they share
a sworn refusal to let
the late-summer day die

fathers   (as if to join the game)
hold out their arms and smile
          shout
                    laugh

but the children know it is a trap
to scoop them up and take them home
          give them food and baths
to warm them up
                    and calm them down

so they run away, diving and rolling
on the fish-breath sand, shrieking
and swooping with the rowdy gulls
          at the edge of the clamoring waves

just beyond the outstretched reach
          of waning daylight

and one last time

La La La the Life Goes On

Obladi Oblada—Lennon & McCartney

between my clapboard garage
and the buzz-cut lawn next door
a house finch graces the fence
effusive song interweaving
with tendrils of clematis
rehearsing for their autumn debut

one of this year's squirrel crop
dive-bombs the bird feeder
from a pine bough above
like a cat, four paws extended

earthward, chases the others
in run-on sentences to keep
the shaken-loose sunflower
seeds and millet for itself

a female cardinal in mottled
camo clutches a red maple branch
calling *here, here,* to reassure
her scarlet mate their speckled
eggs are safe

I sit on the back steps, mug
of tea in hand, a thin scrim
of tranquility settling into
my spine, my breath, my eyes

after the neighbor's fat black cat
crossed my path this morning
a dove's last flutter suspended
from its teeth, gray feathers
scattered on the grass

we all try our best to forget, but
at dusk, a lone mourning dove
will still be waiting on the ridgeline
of the neighbor's house, cooing
softly to herself, dressed in tan
and gray and grief

IV. FALL

The Dilemma Regarding the Murderous Black Cat

I know I should be tolerant
of the black cat's claws
their stark precision
as she leaps from the dark
lattice of boxwood branches

but instead I imagine
the arc of the rock I would
hurl at her twitching tail

I know I should accept
the piercing sharpness
of teeth sunk into a nuthatch
neck, the heap of gray
feathers she leaves behind
like a poor man's gravesite

but I find myself conjuring
a snare to hog-tie her legs

I know I should admire
the cool fire in her amber eyes
as she proudly ambles off
the weight of a dove
in her jaws, slowing her pace

but I envision the unerring
flight of an arrow

I know she's just doing
her job in the ebb and flow
the inevitable interweave
of life and death

but I relish the time she dropped
a catbird and ran in panic
to the copse of brambles
across the street when I yelled
what the fuck

I was sure the limp gray bird
was dead as he lay there
but he rose, shook cat-spit
off his wings, flitted to safety
in the hemlock's nodding
boughs, and sat practicing
the sudden bark of my voice

Metamorphosis

behind a scrim of mist
aspens whisper to each other
in hurried hieroglyphics

I cannot translate or transcribe
their prattling, the pages
of my mind unlined, blank

I sense more kinship
with this rapt orange eft—
motionless in yellow leaves
at my feet—who believes

I am a gnarled sycamore
thirty fathoms tall
two hundred years old

soon to be consumed
by fire that gives me leave
to reseed and begin anew
as a sapling, awaiting

knotholes and lovers'
hopeful hearts chiseled
in my mottled bark

in time, the flame-hued eft
will give up its leaf-lined
forest floor and become

a newt, weave its way
through putrescent pond scum
in stippled green skin

I will be gone, but aspens
will carry on at the water's edge
spreading rumors underground

Heirloom

I saw you stretch so eagerly
from earth to stem
to acrid yellow flower
no bigger than the nipple
on a baby's breast

so when you bore a solitary
green orb, I nurtured you
with care, wet-nursed
with nightly spray

kept at bay the eyes
of wayward rabbit
mandible of voracious fly
and thunder's clumsy hand

until I brought inside
your offspring, primed
to go alone, to ripen
on the kitchen windowsill

now you stand here, barren
save for one forlorn and
hopeful bloom, too late
too close to the deadly
breath of winter

no longer any worth to me
you drain the earth beneath
your tangled toes of nutrients

that feed your sister next to you
still strong, still birthing tiny
golden globes that burst
like sun on fading leaves

yet I hesitate to yank you up
by roots that reared a single
fruit, knowing it would be
sacrificed, emerald flesh
and luscious nectar, to sate
my patient, watchful hunger

Anasazi

I planted Anasazi beans, the ones
you gave me in the last brilliant
days, cool nights of May

they are ancient, you said, sacred
they come from desert pueblos
russet mesas burned by infinite
turning, the unseen wheel of time

in my hand, they sang the songs
of their spirit home, clad in maize
burnished calico and cream

I planted them in earth black
as Anasazi eyes, touched them
once a week with water, just
enough to ease their parching

spindly threads enchanted
summer clouds, the blue
of June, flourished, green
and sinewed, wrestled roses
and tomatoes to the ground

still they sought the sere
expanse, the hard demanding
light of desert days, clarity
of desert nights, ancestral home

so I planted sticks beside them
helped them pray, proud and
straight, to the corn mother
to dry arroyos of their dreams

and far from the scent of scrub
pine, of sagebrush, the austerity
of distant mountains, they
sprouted perfect flowers, hardy
and determined in the warmth
of their adopted soil

yet in September's waning days
October's knife-sharp chill, I
could not slake their loneliness

leaves began to fall, stems
began to fail, turn to brown
drop to black earth that did
its best to nurture them

and their calico children never came

empty-handed in the fading
autumn light, I tried to tell you
but you too were gone

Symbiosis

throughout the summer, I clipped
dead flower heads, nurtured
new ones, enticed with purple
indolence the lingering wings
of fritillaries, skippers, sulfurs
painted ladies, swallowtails
even an occasional monarch

daily, they graced the bush
blessed it with delicate flutter
swoop and glide, young girls
slow-dancing in the sleepy sun

and honey bees, uniformed
in gold and black, embraced
each floret with the hunger
of young love, zigzag arrows
counterpoint to the languid
drift of butterflies

now they are all gone, none
faithful to the final flower
the one without a partner
in the pas de deux of stamen
nectar and survival
save for a single

bumble bee, unmoving, head
buried in the sticky sweetness
of the flower's inner heart
perhaps already dead

I stroke a wing, he moves
a leg, waving me off, and
when I touch his thorax
he nods, still nestled
in the fading essence
of the tiny temptress

there he will remain, waiting
for first frost, content
to die in the comfort
of his lover's wizened arms

Praying Mantis

she clings to the window screen
like a pole dancer, glancing
seductively over her slim
green shoulder at me
with ET eyes
                    wonders
why I watch so closely
from the other side
        of rippled glass

I tell her I just came in
from clipping the last leaves
of mint before the dead
        of winter sets in

and rosemary and thyme

she keeps her serrate forelegs
        folded like hands
in a Dürer print, her days
of rapacious predation
behind her, as a sun-dazed
                    fly saunters by

she has done what needs
to be done, laid her eggs
in a sac that will harden
to ward off frost and snow

and now she waits

by spring when her two
hundred babies are born
she'll be gone, at best
a desiccated statue still
clinging to the window sill

I ask her what
is the god
                    she prays to

she does not choose
                                        to answer

Ladybug

among brown leaves
of oak, gilded fire
of maple in the still-
        green grass

                halfway
up a stalk, a scout
searching the gray
horizon for signs of
enemy smoke and rage
                she sits

a crimson drop
        of fresh blood

I brush by
        with a fingertip

she does not move

apparently her tiny
                life is over

last night an icy chill
a clear black sky
a brilliant moon, full

today
        a new shadow
on your lung

not to worry, the doctor
        says

                it may
be nothing

How to Birth a Perfect Pear

look for bruises that have not yet blossomed
check for shriveling just under the stem
or a subtle softness that portends a wound
where the flower fell off the swelling ovule

bring it to your nose and search closely
          for its future perfume

feel for that firmness with the slightest give
that will turn to fragrant honey on your tongue
          in exactly three days (or four)

thank the bees for brushing accidental legs
on pistil and stamen as if they could foresee
the voluptuous shape to come

cradle it in your hands on the way home
like a full house in a poker game
          or a fitfully sleeping child

do not let it fall as you place it
on the south-facing kitchen windowsill

remember the one time you thought making love
in a meadow in August really would lead
          directly from now to forever

maintain a daily vigil for incursions
by a parade of ants and small children
until you are quite sure it is ready
                    for the knife

Second Chance

I don't know why the doublefile
viburnum has decided to lay out

a new crop of blossoms this week
on a backdrop of maroon leaves

about to fall except it's 73 degrees
and sunny today and has been

all week and maybe the woody
old bush figured *what the hell*

might as well try once more
before frost shuts me down

remembering spring buds sprayed
with capsicum to keep squirrels

from gobbling them all before
they had a chance to challenge

the chill winds and late sleet of April
and after that blooms didn't really

come on in full force so maybe now
since it's been so hot probably

from too much CO2 the leaves
are determined to hold on

and juice still pumps up through
the cambium to give twigs one last

chance to remind fat squirrels
and November's leaf-mold breath

who really runs the show so *what*
the hell the ancient creature reckons

branches wagging in the breathy breeze
if this is global warming, bring it on

Raking Leaves

in autumn air crisp
          as a Granny Smith
                    a taste
of incipient snow

in fallen leaves
                    pages
of a red maple's journal:

travelogue of frenetic
          leaps of squirrels
branch
                    to branch

          a robin's nest
left since spring
                    to blow away

in the rhythm
          of my rake
the sibilance
          of memory:

when the pile was
          high enough
we all dove
                    headfirst

          into the dusty
brown mound
                    shrieking
          gleeful

then came
          a father's feigned
disapproval   the orange

rage of the fire
the pyre of maple
oak
beech

little demons dancing
in the glow

and at sunset
blackened earth
the smell
of acrid smoke
in our tangled hair

and the lingering tingle
of feral frenzy

Incantations

1. Felling Ash

select the one with the most
military bearing—straight, tall—
that calls for both arms to reach
to full extent around its girth
and solitary enough to assure
that its fall to earth does not rip
the lower limbs of its neighbors
out of their sockets

tell it tales of beautiful bats
and hockey sticks—smooth
straight-grained and strong
wielded against all odds—
that will be born of its steady
trunk and massive leaders, then

lead with the bite of a singing
ax swung from the hip, carving
at its feet a clean fifteen-degree
wedge to foretell the pathway
of its crash-and-thudding fall

now turn to the high side
and swing for the fences or a
slap shot on goal, over and over—
rhythmic and merciless—until
the ringing song of metal on wood
yields to crack and twist
of fibers giving way, letting go

falling to final rest on leaf, copse
and loam at your quaking feet

2. Splitting Maple

let the variegated rings be known

let them sing to you the history
of nascent branch and knotted limb
of ceaseless rain and parching sun
seek out the sutured scars of ancient
lightning strike or purifying fire

let the veins born of desiccation
and dimming memories of lifeblood
speak in meandering voice through
ring after ring, year upon year
let them be the guide of your steady
surgeon's hand, your discerning eye
O gentle hooded executioner

heed the silent signs, memorize them
and you will be rewarded well
for a single cracking thud cleaving
clean through xylem and phloem
leading to the least amount of pain
and bleeding and only the subtlest
of muffled creaks and groans

yes, you will be rewarded well
in whispered smoke and flaming
fingers in the chill shadows
of winter's darkness

and as your willing acolytes ebb
and fade to softly pulsing embers
they will bring you waves
of warmth and fevered visions

the gentle compassion of their dying breath

3. Stacking Oak

you must talk to them, each piece
release them from familiar place
in trunk or phantom limb

free them of their fading memory
of leaf and flower, acorn, seed
read in careful tones the history
of their life in grain and knothole
bark, twist, and burl

acquaint them with their new
companions, united not
by annulus or cambium
but by fit and comfort on the pile

full contact in their resting place
nested in among the others
anchored in forbearing earth

tell them softly of coming rains
slashing sleet and snow
the huddling they will need
together against icy wind

until the great reward to come
inseparably bound in flame
and coal, ember, ash, and smoke
remembered long in gratitude
for bringing primal warmth
and flickering glow to the depth
and dread of winter

When November Comes, My Garden Cultivates Wishful Thinking

today there is the loamy
breath of spring, the little
deaths of raindrops
on the sidewalk

garlic bulbs I planted
in October insist on birthing
tender shoots like hands
in prayer, blithely denying
the prospect of an ice storm

oregano persists as well
sporting petite pungent leaves
in vain hope of a glimpse
of hot noon sun

thyme weaves threads
into the neighborhood
of stones, commingles
with the spindly legs
of lavender

only the rangy spearmint
is dressed in tacit twigs
ready for the dreamless
sleep of winter

while leaves of maple
huddle among weeds
like bodies of refugees
prepared for burial
under a quilt of snow

Thanksgiving Day

this little stream speaks
the language of rainy
highways and subway
trains deep in the distance
of a dripping tunnel

its skin glows, flickers
in the afternoon sun, touched
by the mind of Midas

raspberry canes, planning
next year's fruit, burn
translucent red to rival
the bush where Moses felt
the voice wash over him

a yearling and a doe appear
from behind the door
of dry autumnal earth

on the bank, a woman sits
on a musty log among
the rocks, cigarette in hand

we have them all over
our yard, she says

doe and fawn seep back
into the space between
leaf and trunk

the sun pulls a cloud over
its fading face, the stream
stumbles off in another direction

all over our yard

Harvest (December 13)

rose hips yield reluctantly
to a tug around their necks

a thorn sunk in a finger
furrows in a bare forearm
the price, blood for blood
of the ruby beads, so
beautiful in brandy or tart
in homemade jam

and they all sing:
winter coats are all the rage
            today in Vegas

stately stalks of mullein
are gentler to the touch
wild cherry bark fights back
a little more but not as hard
as rose hips do, no tattoos
left to heal on gloveless hands

while a fleece would be too much
            for me to bear

atop the hill, soft brilliance shines
in a cloudless sky worthy
of the woven gold of haystacks

winter coats are all the rage
today in Vegas, while a fleece
would be too much for me to bear

and still no snow
            in Buffalo this year

Wednesday (Winter Solstice)

sparrows wait
politely on a wire
puffed up
in winter coats
like whole notes
on a treble clef

fat squirrels
insist on loopy
figure eights
across the face
of the frozen lawn

while three logs
sit in wonder in
disappearing snow
waiting to be split

or set as anchors
in the mind
of a zen garden
come spring

V. EPILOGUE

Winter Song Cycle

1. Almost Winter

almost winter now
shovel clings to fleeting snow
four geese flying south

2. Chickadees

shortest day has passed
          now it rains
snow breathes
                    softly melts
fog lifts
          softly

only chickadees remain

airplane overhead
          invisible

fog softens
                    no thunder

only chickadees remain
          in tuxedos
await spring
                    softly
fog muffles voices
          to whispers

                    remembering
the sound of dry leaves

3. New Year's Day

is it a new year
because it rains today?

the wind lies down
hides among
wilting grasses

deer, baffled and unsure
wear their winter gray
beside the road
not brown

it is a spring rain
nevertheless

4. Filtered Sunlight

how unfair
the air so translucent
sunlight filtered
through its own pride
eager dew steaming up
from the pavement

do the maples know
not to yawn and stretch out
budding branches?
the forsythia not to dream
of brilliant lemon flowers?

and why does the blue jay
not remember
it is only January?

5. And Yet

snow
        frozen so hard you
                can walk on it
without falling through

a child could jump without a crunch
                (you think)

you walk carefully
        not to break the moment

you say aloud: "I could make an igloo"

it does not fracture the silence

and yet

a cardinal slurs its words
        in a cherry's barren arms

a flock of robins scurries by
in orange and brown overcoats
        bundled against the biting wind

a pileated woodpecker taps
a secret code in a branch
        of a sapless oak

on the scabby elbow of a paper birch
        chickadees gossip raucously

snow
        frozen so hard
not a drip of thaw
                                and yet

6. Third Day of Spring

after all, it is
          the third day of spring

then why are starlings falling
          windblown
from acrid branches of a sugar maple
like leaves that fled in the fall?

and why did it snow today?

perhaps because winter
was softer than a gray spring lamb
          gentle and willowy
                    unsteady on its feet
when we expected the worst

now, the wind roars by
          like a muscle car, tries
not to be just
          a dying thought
beyond the reach
                              of an open eye

but look: a persistent patch of blue
                              nestles
in the stern northwestern sky

Title Index

S

T

W

First Line Index

T

W

Y

www.ingramcontent.com/pod-product-compliance
Lightning Source LLC
LaVergne TN
LVHW030922080826
845145LV00013B/3015

* 9 7 8 1 5 9 4 9 8 2 1 7 0 *